Journey

CW01425797

Ian Nenna

BookLeaf
Publishing

Presentation by *BookLeaf Publishing*

Web: www.bookleafpub.com

E-mail: info@bookleafpub.com

ISBN: 9789357441278

First edition 2023

To my biggest supporters; My mum Pam and my sons Thomas, Christopher, Stephen and Mark. Your unwavering support and love has fuelled me and made me appreciate all I have.

To my university lecturer at LIPA Brendon Burns, thank you for seeing what I often neglected to see and for continuously encouraging me.

And finally to dad, taken far too soon and missed so much more than I could possibly say. I hope I make you proud.

PREFACE

I recall that I moved (with my family, due to my young age) to what was then the Ford Estate (now the Beechwood) in 1971. From the 'Avenues' of the North End of Birkenhead, the pre-war two up two down damp, cold, coal heated, outside loo mid terrace house I took the short journey to what was to become my new modern, family friendly, blank canvased, all local amenities provided (including five pubs) home.

I remember staring in awe through a six year old eyes (my eyes that is, not some grizzly horror movie inspired spectacles made from the globular organs of a neighbours offspring) at what was to me, a palace of opportunities within a shiny new world. The estate however like Christmas presents come boxing day soon lost its appeal when, like many other estates in the seventies and early eighties it attracted its fair share of problems from drugs, anti social behaviour, vandalism, neglect, bad planning and oh, the occasional riot.

Despite this I had a loving family life, friendships were made, neighbourhoods were established, people took pride in their modern homes and what my mum and dad referred to as 'characters' became a big part of my childhood memories. I feel that I must state at this stage that in the late 1980's funding was provided and the estate received a major facelift. The tatty looking pre fabricated housing was systematically replaced by red brick homes with their own driveways, energy saving windows and renewed optimism... oh, and for some reason, the EU provided the now renamed Beechwood Estate with a cycle path, yeah go figure that one out.

It was during my formative years at the new St. Pauls primary school that I developed my love for reading, something my parents fully encouraged. I was often found under my polyester bed sheets with a torch escaping into the worlds of Enid Blyton, CS Lewis and AA Milne. The stories I greedily ate up became the spark that ignited my young imagination and allowed me, even later in life, to question the world around me.

I have a profound love for my home town of Birkenhead, even though it is severely underfunded and moth bitten. I also have pride for the wider Merseyside area; it's history, people and stories.

I have performed my brand of spoken word poetry at festivals, theatres, on radio, in pubs, back rooms and community halls throughout England and Wales.

The poems in this book not only tell the stories and memories of people who lived on and around the Ford Estate from 1970 to the birth of the 80s but also highlight my passion for the area and my love of imaginative stories.

The Seven Thirty-One

Seven thirty-one,
Bidston to Wrexham borderland train, hobbles
its way
through the dull grey, dreary grey, drab
grey-haze-soaked morning.

Clickity click clack,
clickity click clack,
clickity click clack.
steel wheel upon steel track,
rings through sculpted cast iron and brick
backed bridges that,
carpet silver-red carriages and echo their
passing.

Nowadays, too-few commuters use this line
those who do, will, to an 'nth degree
space themselves throughout the carriage
with a geometrical precision that would provoke
architects and mathematicians alike to glory in
its perfection.

Seven thirty-one is never a time for unsolicited
conversation

so, to avoid the slightest possibility of eye
contact
(the prerequisite of mundane dialogue)
passengers will fidget with cardboard tickets,
reread pages in well-thumbed books,
or carefully pen numbers, one to nine, in line
in newspaper grids.

Sightless, sleep-crust lead laden eyes
will occasionally gaze out of the mist mottled
windows.
Nod-to-the-past, underused, unmanned,
disregarded Stations
will intrude upon unfocussed fields of vision.

Each, near observed timber-built structure,
displays its grimy black and white pictures on
time ragged walls.
Nicotine-dyed, tar bemired galleries, offering up
images of
sepia-stained portly station masters, perfectly
manicured flower beds,
sparkling windows, and bustling ticket offices.

Contrasting against whitewashed walls,
the pristine freshly pressed attire porters,
laden down with parcels and packages of mid
afternoon commuters,

patiently await the passing of Shotton bound
coal train.

Children stare in awe as infinite carriages of
black char rattle their way through and through.
Observant mothers, with the precision of hunting
Kingfishers
pluck their charges from platforms edge
ensuring summer clothes are not polluted with
ballooning coal dust.

Monochrome memories along with the
whitewash have now faded.
As corroded milk churns maintain a ghostly
observance of history,
rust chained wooden signposts offer up an
indication of place.
Town and Village names that as the journey
progresses, become enemy to those
unaccustomed to the Welsh language.

Each Llan, Pif and Cwm ensnares English
tongues, as am Cymry,
whose voices float among the green valleys and
granite hills,
sing tales of generations past.
Cry praise to this lands proud people
Oh! Dw I'n caru Cymru!
Dw I'n caru Cymru!

That but, is the there
and the here is the where we now are,
two minutes from Bidston,
starting line of this cross-border journey.

In the here, we see
tacking together the Fender and Ballantyne,
a single road, a path less travelled even than the
tracks it spans.
Look now, as we consider this solitary,
Dromedary humped, sand-brick bridge.
An innocuous crossing, that once offered
to travellers on blue and cream Birkenhead
corporation busses rumbling towards the shale
and sand shores of Moreton, West Kirby, and
Hoylake,
a stomach lurching drop that came with each
decent of its arched back.

Nowadays, the only intrusion of mass traffic to
this place comes through the resonated whisper
of distant bypass.
Built in the 70's to accommodate a modern
generation of family car owners, career go
getters and package holiday adventurers.
This new age hustling, bustling, busy breed,
would no longer need a scenic, meandering, sit
back and enjoy-the-view excursion.

As if mourning the loss of absent times,
the seven thirty-one train, dopplers its way
towards the not so far-flung Welsh border.
It's clanging wheel on rail melody fades, just as
the duotone
diesel drone
of Ford Transit van fills the void.

Under Beechwood

The milkman
complements dawn chorus with a jingling glass
bottle percussion.
Whistles a contrasting harmony, four-part
melody
to rising voice of Sparrow, Chaffinch, and
Thrush.

Milkman, a rare breed nowadays.
Competing with supermarket almond, soy and
hazelnut
dairy free, lactose free, fat free six-pint
containers
nevertheless, his aim is
to continue in the tradition
of those that came before him.

Ghosts of Express Dairy and Unigate men
will line the route and then
tilt their caps to this guardian - of their trade.

He drops off for Mrs Bibby, at number sixty
her usual milk for cereal and morning tea
before returning to his round and his next
customer…

Two hundred yards down the road.

Pickings here are slim
but to him, that doesn't matter
as his customers are faithful
and he knows every family member by name.

This is the Beechwood Estate
twenty-five minutes to the hour of eight, a.m.

Clock alarms, fifth time on snooze, whose
beeps with an uninvited, unsettling bleep
refuse to let those destined for school
return to deep - slumber.
Mums in unison from the bottom of the stairs
will scream... a Harpy like shout

"Gerrout of bed NOW, or God help me, I'll drag
you out"!

This is the here and now, present day
autumnal morning haze
Illuminates a maze of roads, footpaths and
cul-de-sacs
a matrix that, capillary like
weaves its patterns over what was once; In the
not-too-distant past
a vast collection of cottages, peppercorn
dispersed

alongside the ford which in turn traversed
the Fender River
however
this hamlet was swallowed up forever
through the conceiving of a living, pulsating,
breathing
brick and mortar organ with one solitary artery
concrete highway, single throughway
through which residents and visitors alike
drive, walk, bus and bike
to the world outside of this, isolated place
this, borough council Brigadoon.

Here within the shadow of Bidston hill
whose observatory still watches
as it has for over fifty years
overlooking those who lived here, and
all through that time
as it plotted changing tides of Dee and Mersey
rivers
so too did it bare witness
to the ebb and flow, of those below its lofted
perch.

This is the now.

This 21st Century mix of property letters,
housing association renters

Thatcher era desirers, those right to buyers who fell
under the spell of a conservative enticement
towards ownership
offering a working class one-upmanship
a chance to ascend the social ladder.

As said, Mrs Thatcher

"Every family should have the right to spend their money, after tax, as they wish, and not as the government dictates. Let us extend choice, extend the will to choose and the chance to choose".

So then

What was there to lose?

There was though a time before then, and so
as we rewind our calendars back, to when
this twenty first century domiciliary space
was birthed from a place of rising
socio-economic need
a Cathy Come Home, Up the Junction
two finger salute to the disfunction
of post war social housing.

It was a time of low income shifting family
needs.
The terraced, two up, two down
out of town-centre red soot bricked house
was demanded, a lot less
no longer a young family's idea of Des Res
wanting more than those generations that came
before.
And so it came to pass,
a land of expanding opportunity
the new of modernity.

Calls were answered, wishes responded to
through a council vision, with a singular mission
of constructing a dull, undistinctive Xanadu
disguised as the promised land.

St. Oswald

Church tower.
Ecclesiastical custodian of an idyllic chocolate
box village
whose Sunday carillons ring forth the spirit of its
saintly Nordic namesake,
a man that in life challenged abuse and
maintained a virtuous morality.

This bastion vows always to preserve the council
of history past.
No bells peal here for the mourning of lost
memory
instead, each new dawn reminisces with a
fondness of all its yesterdays
and readies its scribes for the writing of
tomorrows day before.

Each diurnal birth, as it has been for over nine
hundred years
brings forth occasion to thank those who
founded this history-soaked place, and
unlike the dimly lit, candle scented, brick and
wainscoted chapel
upon which stained glass windows project a
faith evoking image

here there is no requirement to kneel for the
summoning of blessed spirits.

For here
you need just close your eyes, arouse still
serenity, and await their arrival.
They will come - to those who wish it.
There, just now… did you feel it?
A shivering piloerection as each small follicle,
from neck to fingertips
peristalsis waves over goose bumped skin.

Welcome forth the spirits of those who once trod
upon this ground
hear their names whispered from granite
markers
dominoed beneath floral garbed bicycle.

Here we stand on Bidston Village Road
A gateway from the then, welcoming in the now
truncating space between old and new.
Here in this timeless space, age is meaningless.

Even if no church stood here, many would still
feel the need to pause
take in
wonder
give thanks.

Glance now if you will
to the white stone farm cottage with its pillar
box sentry standing guard.
This quaint inoffensive building, once a bustling
tavern
served forth eggs and ham that, for visitors and
locals alike
were a feast for the stomach and the soul.

But wait, for this place hides a darker past
a past that that belies its proximity to the church
of virtuous Oswald.
For here the then Ring-O-Bells was whispered in
the same breath at the infamous Mother Redcap
whose walls and cellars provided a place of
hiding for nocturnal entrepreneurs.
Each moon alit merchants goods shuffled along
Wirral's beaches so as to not disturb the poor
overworked customs men.

Stay your mind now and you will hear the songs
and revelries of those
who had succumb to the temptations of the
Ring-O-Bells.

All to soon, the neighbour church would
encourage abstinence upon the village.
Never again will the doors open to drunks,
runners and diners.

Never again will a public house satiate those
living within village boundaries.
But for now, the pigs will provide much sought
after ham
the ale will flow freely, duty free goods will fill
cellars
and the song of the Ring-O-Bells will float over
smugglers tides;

Walk in, my friends and taste my beer and liquor
If your pockets be well stored, you'll find it
comes the quicker;
But for want of that has caused both grief and
sorrow,
Therefore you must pay to-day: I will trust
to-morrow.

Wally and Nora

It was around 1980

They both lived next door to me
number seventy-three
no kids, a cat that's all
she was as big as he was small and
in my mind's eye I still see...
that one image that keeps coming back to me
blue plastic rollers that were in perpetuity
ensconced beneath a nylon headscarf.

There was absolutely no question
not even the slightest suggestion
that she didn't rule that particular roost
with a look that could curdle milk
and size nine Doc Martin boots.

One day, in passing
she said to me:
this self-styled goddess of matriarchy
I don't know what it is,
but there's something about you
something about you
that reminds me of my husband

Oh, okay, really?

Yeah… I don't know what it is

Then, folding arms, leaning back
head slightly… tilted she looked me
up, and, down
through dreary water-logged crow foot eyes
up, and, down
supping morning air through ill-fitting National
Health teeth
up, and, down
puckering market stall bought Tahitian sunset
red lip-stick lips
up, and, down
paused, then...
Yeah – he's an idiot

Hey... what... are you calling me an idiot you
cheeky...
well are you?

Is what I thought.

Never said it, thought it but
letting it lie I blew it off and went on my way.

The thing is you see
the thing - is

between you and me, well
I viewed her husband differently
to how she
described
him.

I recall a quiet friendly timid man
eyes lowered sunken featured face
knowing his place
as he maintained a steady pace
behind her.

This was his life
a downtrodden Wally with his Nora Batty wife.

But no
it wasn't quite the same because the real Nora
well, she had a comedic aim yeah?
But this woman…well
it wasn't quite the same.
For him you see there would at no time ever be
a taste of summer wine.

I knew more than I really should
of how this woman…

You know the walls between the houses
they're you know, well thin
what seem like a paper width apart?

So thin, you could undoubtedly hear
cockroaches' fart
from four doors down.
And that's no exaggeration
bear with me
hear me out
my explanation
of how I heard the constant din
it was her I heard not him - in raised voice
with collection of choice biting words.
It was never an argument
an argument you see is a two-way street
volley and return
people in turn
presenting voice raised opinions.
What did I hear?
okay, well
whatever it was it was very clear that
it was not an exchange of views
but rather a one-sided barraging blitzkrieg
a brutal bombardment
a Weapons grade
pre-empted tirade
homed in and destined to hurt
With an explosion of;
you always
you never
why can't you?
I told you

how could you
are you stupid, well, are you?

Each word hammered home
with reasons why this man
was no man at all.

In my mind still
I see this non-man
this gentle subhuman non-man
quietly cowering
as he tried to appease the towering
threat that forever loomed.

I didn't say a thing it wasn't my place
to participate in their private space.
Back then
what went on behind closed doors
was sacrosanct, inviolable, sacred
untouchable.

So I let it be blew it off turned up my T.V.
blasted out This is Your Life
so I couldn't hear his resentful wife
launch her words of personal destruction.

Anyway, what was there could I say?

We were taught weren't we?

as young lads
that boys are… well, all bad
slugs and snails
wasn't that the phrase?
slugs and snails and puppy dogs' tails
whereas the fairer sex
placed on a pedestal from birth
sugar and spice all things nice
sweetness and light
you must never hit girls
wasn't that right
even if they hit you?

Oh, and while we're at it
one more thing we were told
and boy was it often intoned, that
sticks and stones may break your bones
but words will never hurt.

Fight, hit, always be strong
Just dust yourself down you're fine move on

Fight em, go on, hit em my son
you're a man now
so act like one.

What an absolute pile of steaming...
The truth is words can and do hurt
constant oft repeated remarks

can spark - flames
flames that smolder
burn self-esteem, scorch it to dust until it is no
more.

Words linger, repeat themselves
in the low regarded recesses of your mind
break you down
until one day, you ultimately find
your life is no longer your own.

You can become controlled you see
and believe you me
that's exactly what she…

What she…

I often wonder what happened to Wally.

Shot for the Stars

The clock on the mantle is chiming the hour
breaking the silence that lived with the night
as into the room, old Jim he comes shuffling
draws back the curtains to let in some light.

He picks up a key from a jar on the table
winds up the clock for its marking of time
looks into a mirror; face old and weathered
eyes staring back have long lost their shine.

There on a shelf in a frame, silver plated
a faded picture of Jim with his bride in his arms
those were the days they said love was forever
those were the days that they shot for the stars.

Three years ago she had to leave him forever
all the love that they had couldn't cure her bad
heart
he turned to the bottle to keep things together
it stopped him from thinking and falling apart.

Just before noon to the pub he will wander
wrapped up in a coat that's all frayed at the
seams
stands at the bar, orders his usual

medicinal whiskeys to block out the dreams.

He'll sit in the corner alone in his memories
watches the ice as it melts in the glass
every so often, the locals who see him
will pass him a Teachers and toast to the past.

Just after eleven he'll stagger off homeward
a frail looking sight being lit by the cars
walks through the door, sits down with the
picture
and cries for the days that they shot for the stars.

Like in the Tabloid Press

Is it like one of those in the tabloid press
the ones we read about each day
where crime, and drugs, and vandalisms rife
and ASBO's are a part of everyday life
the ones we read about each day...?
You'd never find us around your way.

And the subject of this debate
that works them up to such a state?
I'll tell you, it's quite simple... mate
I just told them I live on a council estate.

Aww!

They'll make their sounds of pity
and they'll look at me really sad
if told them, hey it's not that bad
they'd pat me on the back and say
there, there, there, everything will be okay
I'm sure one day you'll find a way to get off that
estate.

Tabloids, they've got a lot to answer for
exaggerating all those 'facts' they wield
telling of druggies going door to door to door

Ere mate, you wanna buy some alloy wheels
d'ya want a trackie, some trabs, I've got an
i-phone three
all the latest releases on blu-ray see
just one low price and deliveries free
that Argos mate, it's got nowt on me.

Every morning in the cashpoint line
pajama clad mothers are biding their time
to withdraw their benefits and head off home
clutching tight to their scripts for methadone
drugged up to the eyeballs all skin and bone
selling their bodies for the sake of a line
neglecting their kids as their partners do time
deadbeats all, violent men
we should never let them out
they're scum
they'll do it again.

The tabloids tell of hoodies ruling the streets
running in gangs and all packing heat
drunk on VK and popping pills like sweets
in no go areas for cops on the beat.
Kids with kids having kids of their own
spawning a family before they have grown
then running off to the council to get a flat for a
home.
Raising obese offspring in depravity and sin

just so they can start the whole nasty cycle
again.

The tabloids inform our population
those sitting waiting in anticipation
of receiving their daily information salvation
that these council estates are an abomination
a one stop location for mass immigration.

British jobs for British workers
British jobs for British workers
British jobs for British workers

But not for me mate, I've got a bad back
I'm an alchy, I'm an addict... even me kids are
on smack
I need benefits for essentials you see
my fags, my ale, my widescreen TV
I was born in this country, I've a god given right
to own a Nintendo Wii.

I come from a long line of unemployable
workers
a proud tradition of employment shirkers
blame the bloody immigrants
don't blame me
I can trace my slovenly lineage back to 1673.

Breaking...

We're all living in a country of dwindling wealth
where honesty and morality have been left on
the shelf
where the lesson of the day is take all for
yourself
lead by the example of government itself.
We're ruled by this fear in black and white
keeping us locked up in our homes at night
from this big bad world full of evil packed....

Yeah you know, right?

But its them that write the stories
them that print the papers
them that light the fuse step back and ignite.

Were doomed as a nation
beyond gods' salvation
caught in a world of greed fueled temptation
the country is dying
it's terminally ill
if the terrorists don't get you
Your own kids will.

The sky is falling
lock yourselves away
the sky is falling
it's safer that way

eat their bleak words
digest what they say
live your lives in terror
it's the great British way...

And it's true

It's true

It must be true, because it says so in the tabloid
press.

Sermon to the Church of the White

In the beginning was…
social inequality
class disparity
feeding the daemons -
demonic spirits of rising deficiency and
amongst this hell-born calamity
lived the forgotten generation
birthed as they were to a baby boom nation
whose only chance at salvation
genuflection to gods of expectation
with an anticipation
of no reply.

Here is the why…

In that age
unemployment begat hopelessness
hopelessness begat lethargy
lethargy begat apathy
and apathy called it forth…
and lo it came
besetting a place of indeterminate grey
grey buildings, grey skies
grey people with - dull grey lives.

Sharp as knives
its gospel stabbed forth with piercing cry...
let there be light.

And there
in land of perpetual twilight
on still black wings it delivered
all those false promises
gift wrapped in a technicoloured dream.

Deceits stalked the streets
prophesised to these
the generations lost sheep
and became their ubiquitous creed.

Disciples emerged from this coming
and
In unity, all hailed its ability
to numb fragile hopelessness
erasing emotion as if it never existed.

Universally praised as everyone's friend
this white powdered entity would lend
all too brief respite
ephemeral escape
it was after all an equal-opportunities affliction.

It is written
this particular affliction

went by many names
yet all its non-deplumes meant the same...
spoke of a solitary blood pocked tram track.
There was no escaping the deathlike grasp
of this all-consuming powder
each silence between hits grew louder and
louder as
It screamed against the struggles of captive
sinner.

Open are the arms of the loser
Closed is the mind of the chooser
of this smoldering pin prick kiss
scorching the mind with a transient bliss.

The brokers of this taker of lives
this foil wrapped burnt spoon
and hot knife life
are the deceivers
the car window back street black soul merchants
reinforced door traders of this here and now
resurgence
of zero hope
clinging like tar to those
Who could no longer cope with a hostile life.

And this, is the word of the white.

The Towers

In these towers
footsteps reverberate
climb sparse stairwells
like smoke clambering over entablature
and brickwork of soot encrusted smokestacks.

Sprinkled amidst shotgun echo blasts of closing
doors
the heavy breathed pants of residents who
weighed down with their red and white
bargain filled, no frills, Kwik Save carrier bags
spiral their way ever upward
cursing the "out of order" sign
that's taken permanent residence on the lift door.

There, on the eighth floor
Mr & Mrs Johnstone who, in 1972
with other young families from the North End
agreed to buck the trend
of outside loos, draught friendly windows
coal fires, damp walls
and remembrances of a pre-war – Britain.

We need you! They spoke.
To take up the offer of pastures new, they spoke.

And so
with the promise of Ticky-tacky boxes on
Bidston Hillside
white surgical walls, vinyl grey floors
and a view that overlooks a prefabricated Eden.

What else could they do?

This was the potential for a new life
a modern life
a cleaner, warmer, more economic
no need for a coal pile in this hot air-heated
domicile... life.

Husband and wife set to decorating their
residence
here on this new Ford Estate it is evident that
all carpets match the drapes.
Orange and brown and white, reflect the
glowing light
of their now electric plastic-coal fire.

Although the estate has five pubs of its own
each one of these avant-garde homes
has room for their own private
ship-prowed linoleum topped heaven
a Watney's Party Seven, Advocaat
and Creme de Menthe stocked bar.

As crying boy aggrandises the fresh flock
papered wall
a whimsy menagerie sits atop the Rediffusion
coloured T.V.
their own private porcelain zoo.

However, who knew?

That these towers within a year... or two
upon council's wisdom, a housing officers'
whim
would mix oil and water.
Young families and Elderly couples
side by side in this high rise
regretting the day they ever thought
the eighth floor sounded lovely.

In local news these towers were viewed
by people who eschew this place
as a space, where
Eau-de-urine scents the vestibules.
Eccentric teenagers block the stairs
no cares, given
for residents existing
in their own now private prisons
missing the days that they were living
in the North End.

Yes the houses there were old

yes rattling sash windows let in the cold
but there was nothing nicer
than sitting in front of a real coal fire, in freezing
cold weather
glued to the 16-inch black and white TV
in a place seeped with community.
Community...
something lacking now in these towers.

Empty cider bottle and fag end strewn landings
are not conducive to a neighbourly tête-à-tête.
In the beginning it wasn't like that
doormats proudly offered up a welcome
for all that should call, and for all, on each floor
tenants would with pride, take their time
to mop the community area tiles and
water plants that adorned landing windows.

No more does anybody floral adorn graffiti
scribed walls
those inhospitable halls.
Nowadays the coconut matted greetings
pile up at the bottom of the stairwell
as a warning to those who would dare enter this
space.

Meanwhile

Outside

upon the mud brown green specked grass
that surround these twentieth century modern
towers of Gomorrah and Sodom
sits a burnt-out Austin Princess.
Exposed insides, flame charred paint and flat
tires
impress all the local progenies.
Through childlike fancies
this wreck will become the epitome
of a fort, a corner shop, a submarine
and despite the looming grey
children are content in their play, until
at the end of the day
windows will open at varying heights
coming to life,
as mothers yell in for their tea
Shaun, Amanda or Mike.
Hungry and easy to please
with a Saturday staple
Crispy pancakes, chips and Birds Eye peas.
In trot the soldiers, sailors and shop keep
and worn out by their day
they'll soon seek out their sleep.

At night, as tomorrows generation dream
bedrooms will reflect the gleam
reflect orange and amber glow of lampposts
below their beds.

Galaxies will come to life as this man made light
illuminates falling rain and broken glass on
cracked pavement.
Sirens fill the void, Pandas blue light
slicing the night with its lightning knife.

The distant thump, thump, thump
from neighbouring maisonettes reggae, ska, and
punk
beat their counterculture messages
for the eleven o'clock Weeble drunks
exiting Buccaneer pub.
Ale ragged men spew onto the street
as will their ill judged chip shop treat
even before they reach their own front door.
Jackson Pollocked half-digested steak and
kidney pudding
will marble concrete pathways
as windmill armed men brawl with jacket
pockets
determined to retrieve snagged house keys.

In the morning though these men
they will pay
it's guaranteed.

Mr Johnstone will have to endure a Saturday
a.m. from hell

whilst clinging desperately to the couch on
which he fell
(a poppy print and plywood lifeboat upon a
turbulent sea
of bitter, whiskey and late night chippy)
with throbbing skull, fuzzy felt tongue,
un-focusing eyes
he will fail to block out excited cries of Saturday
kids.
Saturday... again! and what's more
Swap Shop, Flashing Blade, Ivor the Engine will
blast forth
as Roger Taylor accompanies inside his head
Sending him back to his lifeboat bed.

As for Mrs Johnstone… well
she will unleash her own kind of hell.
As her poor poor, buffalo snore
Newcastle brown scented man about town-
lays, oblivious
was about to discover the ode
revenge is an angry wife's dish best served cold.

She won't need to speak
But she will if woe betide, he doesn't eat.
Her reckoning will indeed be sweet
Cold egg, cold sausage, cold black pudding
with cold fried bread in cold bacon grease.

At Night

I twist
sheets, skin, mind

Time drags

s t r e t c h e s

slows down through treacle spoon drips

drip

    drip

      drips

echoes into the darkness.

Caved midnight pitch and tar blind mans buff
black.

Wretch, claw, rip... break out!

This is the inside me

the thinking me
the fearful me

Hate filled, angry

I despise...

I left myself a message
a reminder for morning
written in hope.

REM

Through a haze of promises
I fall
into a deep quiescent state
seeking, ultimate sleep.

Come,
wrap me in lifeless
isolation.

Take this dark scowl
this unnecessary
superfluous
excess of mortality.

For I crave solitude.

A blissful
empty
void.

Guide me away from the pain of
thought and...

Unwanted distractions
of this ambiguous life.

On Eden's Mirror

The woods whisper of intrusion.
Beneath a green shroud refuge
cautious feet tread,
search an enclosed spot;
Serene
placid
waiting.

Softly snapped bracken heralds,
echoes the moss.
A collared dove cries forth it's arrival
seizes a tumbling cloud
vanishes
misting through the fabric.

Coppice stares.

Cautious hands
tease bramble and gorse
encourage pathways
conceive a private space
within solitudes gateway
this unseen haven.

Eyes of others are not welcome
for here,
voyeurism is reserved for the trees.

Did

Did his father expect to see
the boy he'd sat upon his knee
full of pride with loving stare
safe within this strong man's care.

Did his mother expect to hear
her babies cry so loud and clear
calling for this woman fair
to soothe his pain and stroke his hair.

Did his parents expect their boy
full of life and boundless joy
to run to them with arms held high
to lift him soaring to the sky.

Did they know he'd make a stand
for love of them in a far off land
and pray one day his task would cease
to change this world from war to peace.

Did he know of parents fears
fathers worry, mother's tears
waiting for the news to say
their child was coming home today.

Did life conspire to cause such woe
when fortunes changed to make it so
this lasting sorrow where once was joy
in silk draped coffin, their baby boy.

Bench

On a hill it sits
Moulded from iron by human hands
Bolted to the granite rock, that in its turn has
also been moulded by the hands of millennia.

There is nothing impressive about this plain,
black, paint peeling bench however, once you
rest upon its cold hard surface; conscience is
transformed, senses are awakened... life is
revealed.

The breeze weaves its winding course. Midges
dart in and out of the arthritic bracken fighting
against the constant threat of being abducted by
sporadic gusts.

Pirouetting throughout the undergrowth the
rousing wind harmonises with soft reed-breath
voices of disturbed leaves.
Accompanied by the sweet pure notes of
Thrushes and Sparrows, whose melodies and
counter melodies add colour to this woven
tapestry, the harsh guttural stabbings of Crow
and Magpie abruptly cut into this scene,
threatening to shatter the melody like glass. In

this theatre however their bullying cries only
serve to add to the opera.

In the unobserved distance timid crickets mark
the tempo, tap the beat of nature, colouring
further still the unveiling pattern.

I am lost in this symphony, encased in its soft
down filled warmth.
The distant rumbling of West Kirby bound train
is but a fleeting annoyance; a cough in this, a
performance of master musicians.

Flies and beetles land as I write my musings.
Iridescent wings prism upon virgin white paper,
shimmering with greens, reds and blues. Just as
it seems I am becoming hypnotised by this
kaleidoscopic performance, drawn into its world
of reflective colour, they take to the breeze and
disappear, buzzing a lament of farewell as they
go.
Although briefly saddened by their departure I
joy at the blessing by their welcome.

My eyes are dragged towards the dull grey
picture in the distance. The cold steel and soot
red bricks of the docks and warehouses
seize my senses and attempt to drag me back
harsh reality.

The hill as if noticing this intrusion, erupts into a fireball of oranges and yellows as gauze bushes explode into life; eclipsing all greys and blacks of human mediocrity. This explosion guide's me back towards serenity; nourishing my soul with it's natural beauty.

I sit content for all too short a time before I force my body to rise and continue on my journey.

Hover flies and cabbage whites conspire to shepherd me back to my place of solitude however, I cannot linger too long for if I do my imperfect humanity will infect the pureness on this place.

I shall be back tomorrow, or the next day for, although it is only an bench, bolted to a hill - it is here that nature sings.

Charge of the Sale Brigade

Half a pace, half a nudge, half a step forward
Dawn of the winter sales lined the six hundred
False teeth chattering, hair dyed blue
Sticks and brollies blocking the path
Keeping their place in the queue

Nervously waiting this eager six hundred
Sanatogen fuelled this anxious six hundred

When suddenly, in unison, they looked at the
clock
Clutching their handbags and hitching their
frocks
As the doorman's keys turned in the locks

ONWARD, ONWARD, ONWARD THEY GO
Surgical stockings, curlers and Scholl

Through the doors they come crashing
A deafening sound
As eager eyes scan this now battle ground

Bargains to the left of them, reductions to the
right of them
Thousands of items are stacked all about

Punching and shoving, scratching and pulling
Wigs ripped off and false teeth knocked out

Look! Look! There on that shelf
Lily of the valley at only one pound
But the shopper who shouted, realised she had
blundered
As a well aimed scone knocked her down to the
ground
Clinging now to a counter, bruised and battered
Stemming the blood that flows from her head
Wishing she had listened, to her husband who
told her
Stay at home Marjorie, watch this morning
instead

Move, move you silly cow, I saw it first, I'll
scratch your eyes
Don't be daft, look at it woman
You're the size of a blimp; it's never your size

There's was not to grin and smile
Theirs was but to check the style
Load their baskets and buy buy buy
Towards the till charged the six hundred

Empty shelves to the left of them
Discarded boxes to the right of them
Wounded shoppers to the rear of them

Out of their sales to their busses they ran
Out of this shopper's hell
Savings been made and savings made well
Charged the six hundred
As onto the credit and store cards, they charged.

Regrets

Be all that you can
To yourself be true
For those you love
Refrain from lies
Regrets you see are eternal yet
We all live ephemeral lives.

Iron

It was the making of Birkenhead
The seed from which the town blossomed.

It was one with the Mersey
a symbiotic relationship of want and need.
The rivers flow gave course and direction
reason and purpose
fuelled it existence
and in return
the Mersey was given the iron it needed...
Floating iron!

Now the iron is all but gone...
the Mersey is anaemic.

The once bustling yards and workshops have
been silenced. No more do the shipwrights,
welders and engineers ply their art. No more do
the dockworkers, longshoremen and stevedores
sing songs of labour.

Waterfront housing has now replaced the
machine droning warehouses and oil fragrance
engine shops.

Dock facing apartments that could never have
been affordable to those men who once worked
here.
Men who grafted through twelve hour days to
keep their families in dock cottages. Generations
of men, women and children born to the river
they served.

Deserted slipways, once surrounded by cheering
crowds, thousands of people
waving with pride as their townsmen's
endeavours took to the river;
Ark Royal, Exmouth, Ajax,
Cambletown, Mauretania and Birkenhead...
Proud names built by the proud men of a proud
town.
A town of Dockers.

A town of shipbuilders.

A town of purpose.

All that remains are the blocked arteries where
the rivers blood once flowed.
Rusted cranes bend over, a stooped reminder of
better, more prosperous times.
Like arthritic hands, deformed joints, they reach
to the Mersey with a hope that she will return
life to their aged bones alas, like all aged men

they are destined to history.

Birkenhead's heart has stopped.

Seduction

Sun drifts on a chardonnay haze,
reflects the bottle green
upon pale skin,
casts long shadows off breathless peaks
dews the valley.

Cooled air kisses flushed red lips,
licks droplets of grape,
and swallows the moment.

Flesh brushes....

tender flesh.

Peregrine fingers explore,
reaching inside
bringing forth soft tears,
arched form,
and gentle sighs from bitten lip.

Teased to no return
he is absorbed within her
they breathe as one
move as one,
are one

tangled...

flowing...

pulsing...

The Sun sets with a smile.

The Truth

He wasn't a bad lad, not really
When she called him in for tea, he'd scarper, for
a lark
Spend hours with his mates, playin' footy in the
park
then he'd turn up, in his turn ups, when the night
turned dark.

But he wasn't a bad lad.

Dirty shirt, messy hair, cheeky bloody grin
But he wasn't a bad lad… I mean, it was just his
way… just him.
It was his way of having fun!
No matter what he did
Her 14 year old son
It was no matter, of no matter…because
he really loved his mum.

And she loved him
This loving caring mum
And the truth she knew about him
Wasn't the Truth that was in the Sun.

The Truth… The Truth! Read all about it!
Read about the Truth.

I mean, come on now listen
it's exactly as they say
It must be true because after all
I read it every day.

It's the conscience of the working class
Those honest folk like me
Their editorials could a Pulitzer prize
And there's knockers on page three.

There isn't an editor finer
than Calvin MacKenzie it's agreed.
He's an oracle, a prophet, a guiding light... he
removes the need to think
Defending all our civil rights… in righteous
blood stained ink.

No, there isn't an editor finer.

Isn't a Newspaper Finer.

Unless you're working class… left wing… a
football fan… or a miner!

MacKenzie warned us of the danger

It was, after all his job,
To tell truth's about the Liverpool thugs… the
violent tanked up mob.
Out on the ale and out on the rob
Stopping the poor Bobbies from doing their job
Urinating on the medics
Stealing from the dead
"Oy! Mate, don't resuscitate her, pass her up
here, we'll fuck her instead…"
That's what the Sun said.

That's what MacKenzie said.

They emptied two public houses… and then
adding to the cheer
They emptied four Supermarkets, of every drop
of beer
"Start to worry Officer, tell the public to run in
fear
It perfectly obvious to everyone, its crystal
fucking clear
were just pissed up yobs on leppings lane
It's a street party in here".

So, it seems he was a bad lad
he had alcohol in his blood…
Come on now admit it
your cheeky lad
he was no good.

He probably had no ticket… he broke into the
gates, we have plenty of witnesses and every one
states...
It was his fault.
He was guilty, for murdering all his mates.

The public won't believe you
you never will find peace
after all the Sun is backed by the truth Margaret
Thatcher, and the Police.

JFT97

Milton Keynes UK
Ingram Content Group UK Ltd.
UKHW020702091123
432260UK00019B/587

9 789357 441278